No. 82. A Sidewalk Café at Night. The Kröller-Müller State Museum

VAN GOGH

PAINTINGS AND DRAWINGS

A SPECIAL LOAN EXHIBITION

THE METROPOLITAN MUSEUM OF ART

THE ART INSTITUTE OF CHICAGO

1949—1950

On the Cover: No. 78. Sunflowers in a Vase. Lent by V. W. van Gogh

The Metropolitan Museum joins the Art Institute of Chicago in the expression of warm gratitude to the museums and private collectors who have made this exhibition possible. Especial thanks go to the Government of the Netherlands, which has graciously consented to lend many fine paintings from the splendid collection of the Kröller-Müller State Museum, through the kind offices of Dr. H. J. Reinink, the Secretary-General of the Dutch Ministry of Education, and of the Director, Mr. A. M. W. J. Hammacher. We also wish to thank the Muncipal Museum in Amsterdam, its Director, Mr. W. J. H. B. Sandberg, and Mr. H. J. Siliakus. Finally, our deepest appreciation goes to Mr. Vincent W. van Gogh of the Van Gogh Foundation, to whom the exhibition owes its inception, and, indeed, much of its realization. In our own country numerous museums and private collectors have been generous lenders, and we acknowledge their assistance with gratitude and the hope that public appreciation of this exhibition will justify their efforts to make it successful.—ROLAND L. REDMOND

LENDERS

CONTENTS

VAN GOGH

ALMOST sixty years have passed since Vincent van Gogh put a bullet into himself, bringing to a sudden close a life of tragedy, privation, and prodigious accomplishment. At his death only a handful of his eight hundred paintings and nine hundred drawings, all done in a period of less than ten years, had been exhibited. Only one canvas had been sold, and only one critic had written enthusiastically of his art.

So clearly did his career dramatize the separation of the artist from society that it was not long before Van Gogh became the martyr of modern art. The remarkable letters he wrote to his brother Theo, in which he poured out his most intimate thoughts, theories, and disappointments, fed the legend. Van Gogh emerged the archetype of the romantic artist as the nineteenth century conceived him: a lonely man, working in poverty and misunderstanding so that future generations could take him to their hearts and cry, "Here is a neglected genius." Ultimately drama turned into melodrama as every shred of Vincent's life was dragged forth and exploited. Novelists distorted his story; psychiatrists fought over the exact diagnosis of his madness. The artist was in danger of disappearing altogether, his paintings and drawings turned into mere illustrations for popular biography.

A certain logic lay behind these biographical excesses. No art is more immediately personal than Van Gogh's. Not only did Vincent look in the mirror again and again and paint his own features; in a sense everything he did turned into a self-portrait —landscape, still life, and figure, into which he injected himself, inventing a new handwriting of line and color to record his intense feelings before nature. What his eye revealed was instantly blended with what he felt about his subject. Increasingly he tried to reduce the interval between vision and execution. The whole was to be done at a flash, artist and nature, mood and design, fused into a tense, expressive unity.

It is easy to read in almost every work the artist's emotional temperature at the time it was made. The dark, lonely drawing of his father's garden at Nuenen in winter (ill. p. 27) springs from a period of subjective gloom. When he reached Arles and felt the enormous impact of southern sun and color, his palette takes on a new splendor while his plowed ribbons of paint betray an almost hectic agitation. In Saint-Rémy, shut away in an asylum with the insane, he paints the gray and desolate view seen through the "iron bars" of his captivity.

This power to identify himself with the moods of nature came only after years of struggle. No one ever felt more deeply the need to love and be loved. But as Theo wrote of Vincent: "There are two human beings in him, the one extraordinarily gifted, sensitive and gentle, the other selfish and insensitive. I am sure he is his own worst enemy, for he poisons not only the lives of others but also his own life." It was only after Van Gogh had separated himself from his narrow Protestant upbringing, only after he had tried to live like Christ among the coal miners of Belgium and failed, only after family, friends, and the women he loved in vain had turned against him, that he discovered that art could offer a way of life. Vincent clearly understood that art was not "the real life," but it became a powerful substitute for normal human relationships. Only when his tremendous energies were channeled into drawing and painting did he begin to find meaning in his existence. He came to feel "alive" only when he was "slogging" at his work, and even after his mental attacks grew more and more severe his painting represented the only "distraction" from those oncoming terrors.

Rejected by his own environment, Vincent sought out peasants and miners, weavers and outcasts, drawing them with a rough, unwieldy vigor which was often more like the artist than his models. Deliberately he identified himself with the destitute and humble. He wanted to live and work like a peasant; at one time he was haunted by the idea of doing a series of prints to hang in the cottages of the poor, "making figures of the people for the people." Always unhappy in cities, he deserted Paris for the South, "to get away," he said, "from the sight of so many painters who disgusted me as men." In Arles he dreamed of substituting a brotherhood of artists for the brotherhood of men, weaving memories of medieval guilds, Japanese craftsmen, and even the Pre-Raphaelites round his "little yellow house," which he dared hope would become "for everyone the house of light."

All this explains why Vincent worked so hard to become a figure painter. His craving for human associations found its deepest release in painting men and women. With a model before him, most often a simple friend from the poorer classes, Van Gogh could experience for the moment that rapport with another human being which he was so often denied. Figures, he remarked, moved him "to the depths," and he once promised his brother that whenever he painted landscapes there would always be something of the figure in them. In southern France the broad reaches of the Crau and the Camargue around Arles delighted him more than the sea; this country was not less "infinite," yet one felt it was "inhabited."

Often too poor to pay for models and too eccentric to get them to pose for him free, Vincent poured his pent-up feelings about men into landscape and still life. This high-tensioned animism instantly distinguished his work from that of the Impressionists, from whom he learned much. For their lyricism of light and color he offered images charged with violence and love. A composition of old shoes becomes a passionate document; his trees twist and turn; his fields sweep into space; and his suns spin with a peculiarly human vibrancy. "If a man tries to create thoughts instead of children," wrote Vincent in a sudden moment of self-realization, "he is still a part of humanity."

So strong was his will to create, so profound were the ideas he longed to share, that Van Gogh could never accept the prettifying of Dutch life or landscape which made the pictures of Mauve and Israels popular. In place of "sentimental melancholy" he sought "serious sorrow." For aid he returned to the sturdier, deeper traditions of Rembrandt and Ruysdael, seeking character in the most simple and common things. He taught himself to probe reality by strenuous bouts of drawing. "I drew a peasant with a spade as many as five times, a man digging in many different attitudes, a sower twice, and a girl with a broom twice." For the picturesque he substituted the "real," struggling to convey the dark, blunt, and ugly side of Dutch peasant life. But, unlike many realists, Van Gogh was not content to stop with simple description. Gradually he transformed realism into a powerful, symbolic method. In The Potato-Eaters (ill. p. 25) he chose a theme of peasants sitting round a lighted table, eating a meal of potatoes with their hands. The painting is carried out in tones of exaggerated darkness, the pigment laid on ruggedly and half awkwardly to suggest the "harshness" and "coarseness" of peasant life.

At this period Vincent confessed that he was far more interested in form than in color, but it was color which ultimately served best to symbolize emotional states and meanings. Always dependent on nature, in Arles he finally transfigured his realism by the clash and harmony of bright hues. No longer did he try to reproduce exactly what he saw but expressed, arbitrarily and forcibly, what he felt. When he came to paint the Café de Nuit it was through a sharp discord of blood red and various greens that he sought to convey "the terrible passions of humanity." For a while, under Gauguin's influence, he tried to work from memory. Recognizing the role of "imagination" in art he attempted to recall elements from nature and arrange them in patterns of color and line. Such effects, he admitted, became more "mysterious," but he gave up abstraction for a renewed, interior realism in which the very paint seems electric with emotion, dabbed irregularly on the canvas, thick here, unfinished there. Vincent left it at that, touched with the excitement and speed of his compulsive vision. Later, after his mental attacks, the paint grew thinner; applied in short strokes, the color sank to duller harmonies. At the asylum in Saint-Rémy he painted a picture in which the "combination of ochre, red, and green with a greyer shadow over it and black contours produces in a way the feeling of anguish from which some of our companions in misfortune suffer and which is called 'black-red'."

By similar exaggerations of line and form, by elisions and sudden extensions of space, Vincent managed to create a world of agitated movement where a few symbols appear again and again. The "high yellow note" of the southern sun is nowhere more striking than in his sunflowers; in Saint-Rémy, the writhing cypresses and reeling mountains become emotional "equivalents" for his own experience. There is the Sower, for seeding time and growth, the Reaper in the sunburnt wheat fields, for death. "To express hope by some star, the eagerness of a soul by a sunset radiance. Certainly there is nothing in that of stereoscopic realism but is it not something that actually exists?"

His belief in such "actualities" seems to come from a deeper inner conviction, so deep as to be called mystic. In his passionate reactions to nature he recognized a feeling akin to religious ecstasy, just as when in his disturbed mental states he brooded on the infinite and the eternal. While on a walking trip in Holland he relates that from one night to the next he was lost in a dream, so absorbed in the "sad music" of the country round Drenthe that he quite forgot to eat or drink, though he stopped now and then to make drawings along the way. "I have a terrible lucidity at moments," he wrote from Arles, "these days when nature is so beautiful. I am not conscious of myself any more, and the picture comes to me as in a dream." In such trance-like moments he believed that painting could "be comforting as music is comforting." He longed "to paint men and women with that something of the eternal which the halo used to symbolize and we seek to give by actual radiance and vibration of our colors."

"Well, the truth is, we can only make our pictures speak." These words Vincent van Gogh wrote in his last letter, just before he died. In the years since 1890 they have spoken, until today he is the most famous of modern painters. How can one explain the vast hordes of war survivors who stood in patient queues at Paris and London, eager to catch even a glimpse of his work? Why were they there? What were they hoping to find?

Some other painters of his time have receded into history. Year by year Cézanne grows greater, but more remote; Gauguin, whom Vincent loved and venerated, now appears, more often than not, somewhat thinly decorative. Meanwhile Van Gogh's art spreads wider and wider circles of appreciation.

Part of his continuing appeal may lie in his unique ability to suggest those tensions and dislocations under which man lives today. When he painted his portrait of Dr. Gachet with what he called "the heartbroken expression of our time," Vincent struck a chord that still resounds in contemporary feeling. A period that idolizes Dostoevsky and makes a prophet out of Kafka will continue to react to such intense emotions stretched to the breaking point. Though Van Gogh's early influence on twentieth-century painting seemed long ago exhausted, it is significant to find that Picasso's latest work echoes more than a trace of Vincent's violence and to hear of the Spanish artist's avowed admiration for his art. It is less surprising to learn of Sartre's interest; Van Gogh's moral austerity, his grim acceptance of reality and responsibility for action, constitute an almost classical case study for Existentialism.

But beyond the instabilities and disasters of his life there lies something deeper to account for his present reputation. This is the triumph, in his art, over misunderstanding, poverty, and pain. In a period when individualism is at stake and when anonymity everywhere encroaches, Van Gogh's affirmation of personal faith finds ready response. To a confused world his vital images have what he desired above all else: the power to reveal and to console.

DANIEL CATTON RICH

EARLY PERIOD

The career of Vincent van Gogh is one of the shortest in the history of art. He was a painter for only ten years, of which more than half were devoted almost entirely to drawing.

He was born in 1853, and he killed himself when he was thirty-seven years old. His life can be broadly divided into two periods: the first, a period of bitter struggles, failures, and disappointments, when his difficult character, his personal views on life, and his highly original way of seeing were formed. The second, the period of fulfillment when he had mastered his art and was conscious of having done so.

His family was of pure Dutch stock and is recorded in Holland as far back as the sixteenth century. Among his ancestry there were artists and preachers. These two vocations, art and religion, were to dominate his life.

His father was a modest clergyman, lacking talent as a preacher but loved by his parishioners, the least successful of six brothers, among whom were a vice-admiral of the Dutch navy and three prominent art dealers. His mother was the daughter of a well-known bookbinder of The Hague. He seems to have inherited his timidity and his human warmth and generosity from his father. From his mother he took his energy, his obstinacy, and, perhaps, his talent as a writer.

Vincent was born in the village of Groot Zundert in the old Dutch province of Brabant. He was the oldest of six children, three boys and three girls. The early years of his youth in his father's parsonage were very happy, and later in his darkest moments they always came back to him. He was a charming and imaginative child who enjoyed playing with his sisters and brothers in the garden of the parsonage. But even at an early age he already loved to go off by himself and wander among the wheat fields, on the heath, and in the pine woods that surrounded the village. This sensitivity to the poetry of nature never left him.

His parents sent him away to school at a near-by village. Almost nothing is known, however, about his education, except that he must have acquired at this time his unusual taste for reading, which, in spite of his personal isolation, kept him aware of what was going on in the world.

When he was sixteen a profession was chosen for him. It was decided that he should become an art dealer, and his uncle Vincent got him a job in the firm of Goupil, of which he was a partner. This was one of the outstanding firms dealing with contemporary painting, with offices in Paris, The Hague, and London. Vincent was put to work in the Hague branch under the director, Mr. Tersteeg, who gave an excellent report on his work and personality at that time but who later loomed up again and again in his life as a symbol of prejudice, indifference, and even cruelty.

It is during this period that he began the letters to his brother Theo, the last of which was found on him, unfinished, the day he took his life. These letters give such a graphic account of his thoughts and of everything that happened to him and their style is so vivid, so sincere, that they can be said to rank with the great autobiographies of literature.

After three years he was transferred to the London office, where the firm had no gallery but dealt only with other dealers. This was a happy, carefree moment in his life. He was independent, living alone for the first time and in the world's greatest metropolis. He enjoyed his work and all the life he saw around him in the walks he loved to take through the city. He visited the museums of London and studied the great masters of the past, of whom he preferred Rembrandt, Hals, Ruysdael, and the leaders of the British school, Constable, Reynolds, Gainsborough, Turner, and old Crome. He decorated his room with reproductions of his favorite paintings, among them a portrait of Corot, and it was at this time that he began to love and admire the work of Millet, who influenced him throughout his life.

He read a great deal: first the Bible, from which he quoted frequently in his letters, but also the poets, and Michelet, Renan, and Dickens, who were to have a profound influence on his thinking. In their writings he found the source for his ideas about the influences that had sprung from the French Revolution, the new social justice, in short, the practice of a true rather than an official Christian way of life. This sympathy for the new revolutionary ideas had far-reaching effects throughout his life. It dominated his theories about art, the position of artists in society, and the way in which they should work together, and it was one of the chief causes of disagreement with his family and their friends.

It was in London that he fell in love for the first time. Each of Vincent's contacts with women had a fundamental effect upon his character, and this initial experience was a turning point in his life. The girl he had chosen, the daughter of his landlady, refused him. This was the first thwarting of his burning desire for human affection, and it seems to have caused a change in his whole personality. He withdrew into himself, became taciturn and unapproachable. People began to speak of his eccentricity. The loneliness that was never to leave him began, and to escape it he concentrated on religion, which seemed to provide an answer to his longing to give himself to his fellow men.

His employers transferred him to Paris in the hope that the change might make him forget his grief and bring him back to his former self. But in his new state of mind the atmosphere of a fashionable picture gallery was most distasteful to him. Taking a small room in Montmartre, he spent his evenings reading the Bible with a young Englishman, a boarder in the same house, his Sundays visiting the Louvre and Luxembourg museums. He still read a great deal, especially the poets Victor Hugo, Alfred de Musset, Longfellow, Heine, Keats. But his thoughts turned more and more away from art and towards religion. His interpretation of the books he read was religious—he destroyed what he had by Michelet and Renan and advised his brother to do the same lest he be led into temptation. The reproductions he had in his room were all of religious subjects, The Bible Lecture, The Imitation of Jesus Christ. He greatly admired his father and wanted to devote himself to bringing comfort through religion to the poor and miserable.

Finally he was dismissed by Goupil and Company and found himself without a job and with no clear idea of how to go about carrying out his wish for a life devoted to his fellow men. Through an advertisement he obtained a job as a school teacher, or rather an assistant without salary in a small school located at Ramsgate on the southern coast of England. Instead of teaching, however, he was sent to collect bills from the parents of the pupils in London. After a while he moved to another school, where he acted as a curate and did some preaching.

He still took some interest in art and visited Hampton Court, where he was particularly struck by the works of Rembrandt, Titian, and Mantegna. But he concentrated almost entirely on religion and became obsessed with thoughts of the sorrow and grief in the world. This was probably increased by his visits to the poverty-stricken quarters of London, where life was reduced to its lowest and drabbest. He also suffered from homesickness and loneliness and, perhaps as a result of this, began to neglect his health. He ate very little, smoked a lot, and imposed hardships upon himself, such as walking from the channel coast to London, a distance which normally takes over four hours by train. But in spite of all this he kept his sensitivity to the beauty of nature and wrote charming and poetic descriptions of what he saw to his family—the dawn near Canterbury, a storm on the channel, a view of a village in a valley which reminded him of a Dürer water color.

Realizing that there was no future in what he was doing, he returned to Holland and with the help of one of his uncles got work in a bookshop at Dordrecht. But he had now made up his mind to become a preacher and made arrangements to prepare for the entrance examination to the university, where he could study theology. He moved to Amsterdam for this purpose and lived with his uncle who was commandant of the Navy Yard. This new attempt to find a direction for his life, however, was also doomed to failure. In spite of his unusual vitality, persistence, and self-discipline, he proved entirely incapable of concentration on Greek, Latin, and the other subjects required of him. In addition to this he found himself totally opposed to the official church way of thinking about and carrying on the teachings of Christ. He considered this hypocritical and hopelessly bound by outmoded customs and prejudice. He wanted not to talk but to act according to the basic teachings of Christ. During this period he copied the *Imitation of Christ* by Thomas à Kempis and read Lamennais, who had himself gone through a very similar crisis. As was inevitable, it ended in a breakdown, and he did not take the examinations.

This second major failure in his life had important consequences for him. It marked a fundamental change in his ideas about religion, and it separated him further from his family, not only from his uncles, who had now lost all confidence in him, but, what was much more painful to him, from his father, with whom he now found himself in almost complete and hopeless disagreement.

In spite of everything, with characteristic obstinacy, he still wanted to become a preacher. But it had to be through action, not through words and theories, and so he entered an evangelical school in Brussels where young men were prepared for missionary work among the miners in the Borinage district of Belgium. Here again, however, although he was much more advanced than the other pupils, his eccentricity, his lack of facility as a speaker, and, most of all, his rebellion against officially accepted ideas prevented his receiving a nomination. Nevertheless he went to the mining region at his own risk and began working among the poor, teaching the children and lecturing on the Bible. He did everything to share the life of the miners, went down into the most dangerous pit, stayed with them constantly. The Evangelical Committee gave him a temporary appointment and at first praised his work, especially his care of the sick and wounded after an explosion in one of the mines. After a short time, however, his enthusiasm carried him too far; he gave away all his personal belongings to the poor and went to live in a primitive hut, ate almost nothing, in short tried to sacrifice everything to the cause he was serving. This was considered an excess of zeal by the Committee, who believed that a man who neglected himself to such an extent could not be a good example for others. When his temporary appointment ended they refused to renew it, and so Vincent once more found himself without a job and, except for his family, with hardly a friend in the world.

In the months that followed, the winter of 1877-1878, he went through the great crisis of his life. Almost completely cut off from his family and his friends, a failure at everything he had tried to do, and, worst of all, having lost his faith, he looked around desperately for some way in which he could be useful to his fellow man; for unless this were possible he saw no reason for his continued existence. At first he went home to his father's parsonage, but, finding himself a stranger there, he returned to the Borinage, spent a dreadful winter of wandering, without work and often without shelter or food, for his family were not always able to send him enough money. During this time he walked many miles to the village of Courrières, where he hoped to consult Jules Breton, a successful artist whose work he admired, but when he got there he did not dare knock at the door. In spite of the depth to which he had fallen he never lost his dignity, never admitted defeat, and even in the worst moments clung to his convictions. Finally he made up his mind to devote his life to painting and through this to bring some happiness, some consolation to humanity. From this moment he regained his confidence in himself. He had a mission in life from which he did not deviate until the day he died.

He began working in the Borinage. His studio was a small room which he rented in the house of a miner, his models the miners themselves, their children, their surroundings. He also copied reproductions after Millet, whose love for the working man he shared, and studied books on perspective. He began to read again, and his letters contain profound reflections on the meaning and interrelation of art and literature.

From this time until the end of his life he received an allowance from his brother, who had become an established art dealer in Paris. Vincent was proud, and this dependence on his brother always weighed on him. He tried to justify it by calling it a business arrangement through which his brother became part owner of everything he painted and by believing that some day he would pay it all back. However, this never really satisfied him and his complete inability to earn anything with his pictures was unquestionably one of the reasons for his final breakdown.

When winter came and it was no longer possible to work out of doors, his quarters in the miner's house became too cramped, and so he moved to Brussels. There he hoped to continue the basic study of anatomy and perspective and above all to get to know other artists, to find what he always wanted so desperately, the warmth of human companionship. He took a few lessons with a painter but failed to make any friends, with the exception of a young Dutch artist called Van Rappard, who was introduced to him by his brother and with whom he later corresponded. After a while, discouraged and worried by the poor state of his health, he decided to return to his father's house.

His father had meanwhile been appointed to another living at Etten, also in Brabant. At home, although he did not get on very well with his family, it cost him nothing and a more regular life helped him to regain his health. During the first months he worked on quietly and contentedly, but soon there arose another crisis, a second unhappy love affair, which was also to have far-reaching effects upon his life. This time he became attached to one of his cousins from Amsterdam, a young widow with a four-year-old son who had come to spend the summer with his family. Vincent was kind to her child, and they became close friends, but when he declared his love she refused him and left the vicarage. He could not believe it and blamed her attitude on the opposition of her family and his. It was only after he went to Amsterdam and she absolutely refused to see him that he lost hope.

The unbalanced intensity of his feeling came out during the visit to Amsterdam. When the girl's family told him of her refusal to see him, he put his hand over an oil lamp and begged that they allow him to speak with her as long as he could hold it there. He could not remember what happened after this. This second frustration of his desire for a woman's tenderness and companionship affected him profoundly. He withdrew completely into himself and became increasingly difficult to live with, until one day after a violent quarrel with his long-suffering father, he left for The Hague.

This break with his family, coming on top of the refusal, made him feel utterly abandoned, and he again went through a desperate period when life did not seem worth living and he almost gave up the struggle. It was at this time that he met a

No. 89. Gauguin's Armchair. V. W. van Gogh

woman who seemed even more miserable and deserted than he. She was a prosti-
tute who had one illegitimate child and was expecting another. He helped her
through the birth of the second child, took her with the children to live with him,
and gave them all the love and tenderness which he had been forced to keep locked
up in his breast for so long.

The illusion of having what he had always wanted, a wife, children, a home,
gave Vincent a new reason for living, and the beginning of their life together was
one of the happiest periods for him. His renewed confidence came out in both his
work and his letters. He arranged and furnished a small studio, hired models,
sketched from life in the town, and worked on landscapes in the surrounding country, on the beaches and in the dunes. He took a few lessons from the painter Anton
Mauve, who was married to one of his cousins. He began painting in water color
and in oil and became interested in lithography, which he believed to be a new
technique of reproduction that would make it possible to bring painting cheaply to
the people. He also read intensively again and kept up his knowledge of what was
going on in the world of art outside of Holland. He collected reproductions of his
favorite artists. The list of these shows his preference for Millet, Daumier, and the
British magazine illustrators, almost always artists whose work contained some sort
of social protest. It was at this time that he first had the idea of organizing a system
of communal living for artists.

Unfortunately this happiness could not last. The woman was of a low type, she
was pock-marked, smoked cigars, and spoke with a coarse accent. Their house was
slovenly, and soon the few people who had come to see Vincent before he took her
in, began to avoid him. Tersteeg, the dealer, who could have been a great help, was
the first to break with him, and he influenced Mauve to do the same. Even Theo,
who was always devoted and patient, showed plainly that he did not like her. Vincent himself felt that something was wrong, for he put off his plan to marry her.
However, with his typical tenacity he refused to admit it and clung to the belief
that her faults were due to her wicked upbringing and that, given better surroundings, she would improve.

Gradually the situation grew worse. Vincent again felt the bitterness of being
isolated. His relationship with the woman was terribly limited since she had no
education at all, and during the long winter evenings he sat alone in his studio longing for the visit of other painters or at least for some place where he could go to
meet them. His funds were always low, and once he had bought his artist's materials
there was little left for the household—sometimes food was so scarce that the poor
woman did not have milk to nurse her baby. This poverty and the influence of her
family, who constantly tried to tempt her back into her former, more lucrative, way
of life, made her restive and upset the home to such a degree that Vincent finally
resigned himself to separating from her and to leaving The Hague. The break affected him deeply. He had loved the woman in spite of her faults, and he was
strongly attached to the children.

Whatever the final outcome, this episode stands out as a symbol of the spirit of Vincent. In it he gave himself completely as he really was, with his desire for a wife and family, his compassion for the poor and the helpless, and his readiness to make any sacrifice to obtain human warmth and tenderness.

He went to Drenthe, a remote village in the peat district, and rented a room in an inn, determined to put the past out of his mind and to lose himself in his work. He wanted to concentrate on the study of peasant types and the landscape of that part of Holland. But he found it difficult to get the peasants to pose. This, his gloomy state of mind, and the fear of falling ill made him change his plans and return once more to his parents' house.

Vincent's father had meanwhile been nominated to another living at Nuenen. In spite of the obvious difficulty of having a painter and an eccentric living in a vicarage his parents took him in and gave him a room to work in. It was an unhappy arrangement, however, for Vincent did nothing to make the relationship easier and avoided all but the most necessary contacts and conversation with his family.

Some months after his arrival his mother fell and broke her leg. Vincent devoted himself to nursing her with the same intensity which he had shown in the Borinage. This brought him closer to his family and relieved the atmosphere somewhat. He became more sociable and began to mingle with their friends. But this was not to last, for it led to another unfortunate love affair. The daughter of a neighbor, one of several sisters whom he saw constantly during the summer, fell in love with Vincent. She was a homely spinster, several years older than he, and, although he did not have as passionate a feeling for her as in his previous experiences, they planned to get married. Her family, however, objected and exerted such pressure that she attempted to commit suicide. This caused a scandal in the village and people avoided coming to the vicarage, which was, of course, embarrassing and distressing to Vincent's family.

He withdrew more completely into himself and spent almost all of his time in a studio he had rented in the village. There the only people he saw were friends such as Van Rappard who were interested in painting. He went to Amsterdam with one of them to visit the Rijksmuseum. His letter to his brother on this occasion, describing the paintings he most admired, the Company of Captain Reynier Reael by Hals and the Jewish Bride by Rembrandt, and stating why he loved the color of the former and the spiritual content of the latter, foreshadow the whole of his later development as a painter.

In March 1885 his father died, and from that time he left the vicarage and lived alone in the studio. He worked there successfully for a while until trouble arose when the Catholic priest forbade his parishioners to pose. In November he left Nuenen for Antwerp, abandoning all his work in the care of a carpenter, who later disposed of it to a junk dealer.

In The Hague Vincent had mastered drawing. In Nuenen he made his first basic progress with paint. He did not yet use his very personal scale of vivid colors. The

studies of peasants and weavers, even the landscapes are painted in somber tones of
brown, blue, and black, which contrast astonishingly with his later work in France.
But his writings show that he was already thinking of the color harmonies that he
later used. His description and analysis of Delacroix's color system could be applied
to any of his own later paintings. This sensitivity was always present in him and re-
peatedly given expression in his letters when he described the colors in landscapes.
That he still suppressed it in his painting was probably due to the influence of
painters such as Millet, Israels, and Mauve, whose palette was subdued.

He painted a series of studies of Brabant peasants at work in the fields and in their
houses. In these he not only successfully defined form in paint but he also began
to concentrate on bringing out those qualities which were most expressive of the
character of his subjects. He emphasized the gnarled hands and block-like features
of the peasants to express the quality of earthiness, and in The Loom he showed the
man as a small ghost-like creature living inside a huge and monstrous machine.

These studies culminated in his first major composition, The Potato-Eaters (ill. p.
25). In this he wanted to give the essence of the Brabant peasant, to show that he
was a "peasant painter." To him this picture was his first achievement; he was proud
of it and sensitive to any criticism. It was due to an ill-advised statement about it
that he broke off his friendship with Van Rappard, his only artist friend.

The move to Antwerp, though it was caused in part by increasing difficulties in
Nuenen, was also a normal stage in Vincent's development as a painter. He wanted
to work in a large center where there would be a greater variety of models and,
above all, where he could meet other painters and learn from them. During his short
stay there he succeeded in doing this. At first he worked alone, hiring his own models
and painting them in his small rented room, which, it is significant to note, was decorated with Japanese prints. As this method of working proved too expensive he began
working at the Academy and at an art students' club where models were available in
the evening. For the first time he found himself among his fellow artists, could com-
pare his work with theirs, sense the great difference between what he did and what
was generally considered good, and hear their criticisms. It must have been a severe
test, but in spite of his feeling of isolation, and of persecution by some of the teach-
ers, he stuck to his beliefs and refused absolutely to conform to the accepted aca-
demic style. Though he by no means considered himself perfect, or even completely
developed as a painter, his personality as he had asserted it in The Potato-Eaters
was formed, and he knew what he wanted.

The conditions in which he had lived and the terrible strain he had put on himself began to tell. He consulted a doctor, who described his condition as near pros-
tration. As a result, and no doubt also because he was drawn to its artistic activities,
Vincent decided to go to Paris, to his brother. He left Antwerp at the end of February. For some unknown reason he took with him almost none of the paintings he
had done there, and to this day the portraits and landscapes of which he speaks in
his letters have never reappeared.

PAINTINGS

ALL ARE IN OIL ON CANVAS UNLESS OTHERWISE NOTED

1. A FISHERMAN ON THE BEACH
H. 19⅝, w. 12⅝ in.
August 1882. De la Faille[1] (H) 6
Lent by the Kröller-Müller State Museum, Otterlo

2. THE LOOM
Illustrated p. 23. H. 27½, w. 33½ in.
May 1884. De la Faille (H) 33
Lent by the Kröller-Müller State Museum, Otterlo

3. POTATO-PLANTING
H. 26, w. 58⅝ in.
August 1884. De la Faille (H) 46
Lent by the Kröller-Müller State Museum, Otterlo

4. A WALK NEAR NUENEN
H. 30¾, w. 38⅝ in.
October 1884. De la Faille (H) 50
Lent by the Boymans Museum, Rotterdam

5. STILL LIFE: HAT AND PIPE
H. 14¾, w. 21 in.
November 1884-April 1885. De la Faille (H) 70
Lent by the Kröller-Müller State Museum, Otterlo

6. A WOMAN IN A RED BONNET
H. 16¾, w. 11⅝ in.
April 1885. De la Faille (H) 159
Lent by V. W. van Gogh, Laren

7. THE POTATO-EATERS
Illustrated p. 25. H. 32¼, w. 44⅞ in.
May 1885. De la Faille (H) pl. I
Lent by V. W. van Gogh, Laren

8. THE OLD TOWER AT NUENEN
H. 24¾, w. 31 in.
May 1885. De la Faille (H) 94
Lent by V. W. van Gogh, Laren

9. STILL LIFE: POTATOES
H. 26, w. 31⅛ in.
October 1885. De la Faille (H) 122
Lent by V. W. van Gogh, Laren

10. THE OPEN BIBLE
H. 25⅝, w. 30¾ in.
October 1885. De la Faille (H) 121
Lent by V. W. van Gogh, Laren

11. A PEASANT WOMAN IN A WHITE CAP
H. 16¾, w. 14 in.
De la Faille (H) 89
Lent by V. W. van Gogh, Laren

12. PORTRAIT OF THE ARTIST
Illustrated p. 24. H. 18⅛, w. 14⅞ in.
1885-1886. De la Faille (H) 188
Lent by V. W. van Gogh, Laren

DRAWINGS

13. THE RETURN OF THE MINERS
Pen and ink on paper; h. 16 15/16, w. 23⅝ in.
August 1880. De la Faille[1] (F) 832
Lent by the Kröller-Müller State Museum, Otterlo

14. A YOUNG PEASANT
Black crayon and water color on paper; h. 18⅛, w. 24 in.
September 1881. De la Faille (F) 851
Lent by the Kröller-Müller State Museum, Otterlo

15. A WOMAN MOURNING
Pencil and pen and ink on paper; h. 22 7/16, w. 16⅛ in.
April 1882. De la Faille (F) 937
Lent by the Kröller-Müller State Museum, Otterlo

[1] The references for paintings are from J. B. de la Faille, *Vincent van Gogh,* Hypérion edition (H), 1939; those for drawings are from de la Faille, *L'Oeuvre de Vincent van Gogh, Catalogue raisonné* (F), 1928, vol. III.

16. THE HAGUE: A CORNER OF THE OLD TOWN
Pen and ink on paper; h. 9 7/16, w. 11 13/16 in.
March 1882. De la Faille (F) 918
Lent by the Kröller-Müller State Museum, Otterlo

17. A STUDY OF A TREE
Crayon, heightened with white, on paper; h. 19 11/16, w. 27 3/16 in.
April 1882. De la Faille (F) 933
Lent by the Kröller-Müller State Museum, Otterlo

18. A FISHERMAN'S HUT AT SCHEVENINGEN
Pencil and pen on paper; h. 11¼, w. 17 5/16 in.
May-June 1882. De la Faille (F) 938
Lent by the Kröller-Müller State Museum, Otterlo

19. BEHIND THE SCHENKWEG, THE HAGUE
Illustrated p. 26. Crayon, heightened with white, on paper; h. 11, w. 18⅛ in.
June 1882. De la Faille (F) 939
Lent by the Kröller-Müller State Museum, Otterlo

20. THE BEZUIDENHOUT PARK, THE HAGUE
Crayon on paper; h. 7 1/16, w. 7½ in.
September 1882. De la Faille (F) 952
Lent by the Kröller-Müller State Museum, Otterlo

21. A VETERAN WITH AN UMBRELLA
Pencil on paper; h. 18½, w. 9 1/16 in.
October 1882. De la Faille (F) 972
Lent by the Kröller-Müller State Museum, Otterlo

22. THE STATE LOTTERY
Water color on paper; h. 14 15/16, w. 22 7/16 in.
October 1882. De la Faille (F) 970
Lent by V. W. van Gogh, Laren

23. AN OLD MAN
Illustrated p. 31. Pencil on paper; h. 18 11/16, w. 10¼ in.
October 1882. De la Faille (F) 960
Lent by V. W. van Gogh, Laren

24. ON THE THRESHOLD OF ETERNITY
Illustrated p. 78. Pencil on paper; h. 19 11/16, w. 12 3/16 in.
November 1882. De la Faille (F) 997
Lent by V. W. van Gogh, Laren

25. A WOMAN SEWING
Pencil on paper; h. 20½, w. 14 in.
March 1883. De la Faille (F) 1026
Lent by the Kröller-Müller State Museum, Otterlo

26. VEGETABLE GARDENS NEAR THE DUNES, THE HAGUE
Illustrated p. 26. Ink and water color on paper; h. 11, w. 16 9/16 in.
June 1883. De la Faille (F) 1037
Lent by the Kröller-Müller State Museum, Otterlo

27. A VIEW AT SCHEVENINGEN
Illustrated p. 27. Pencil, black crayon, water color, and white chalk on paper; h. 17⅛, w. 23⅜ in.
De la Faille (F) 1041
Lent by V. W. van Gogh, Laren

28. A ROAD NEAR LOOSDUINEN
Black crayon and ink, heightened with white, on paper; h. 10¼, w. 13⅞ in.
De la Faille (F) 1089
Lent by V. W. van Gogh, Laren

29. WOMEN PRAYING
Black crayon and pencil on paper; h. 16 15/16, w. 11 7/16 in.
De la Faille (F) 1058
Lent by the Kröller-Müller State Museum, Otterlo

30. A LUMBER SALE
Water color on paper; h. 13 3/16, w. 17 5/16 in.
January 1884. De la Faille (F) 1113
Lent by V. W. van Gogh, Laren

31. THE WEAVER
Water color on paper; h. 13⅜, w. 17¼ in.

January 1884. De la Faille (F) 1107
Lent by V. W. van Gogh, Laren

32. THE GARDEN OF THE NUENEN
     VICARAGE
     Illustrated p. 27. Pen and pencil on paper; h. 15⅜, w. 20⅞ in.
     March 1884. De la Faille (F) 1128
     Lent by V. W. van Gogh, Laren

33. A GARDEN IN WINTER
     Pen and ink on paper; h. 11, w. 8 1/16 in.
     March 1884. De la Faille (F) 1131
     Lent by V. W. van Gogh, Laren

34. STUDIES OF HANDS
     Illustrated p. 29. Black crayon on paper; h. 7⅞, w. 13 in.
     January 1885. De la Faille (F) 1155
     Lent by V. W. van Gogh, Laren

35. A PEASANT WOMAN IN A
     WHITE CAP
     Illustrated p. 28. Black crayon on paper; h. 15¾, w. 13 in.
     February-April 1885. De la Faille (F) 1182
     Lent by V. W. van Gogh, Laren

36. A WOMAN SHELLING PEAS
     Black crayon on paper; h. 16 9/16, w. 10¼ in.
     March 1885. De la Faille (F) 1214
     Lent by V. W. van Gogh, Laren

37. A WOMAN BESIDE THE HEARTH
     Water color on paper; h. 13 9/16, w. 17½ in.
     March 1885. De la Faille (F) 1222
     Lent by V. W. van Gogh, Laren

38. THE DITCH
     Pen and ink, heightened with white, on paper; h. 15⅜, w. 13 in.

De la Faille (F) 1243
Lent by V. W. van Gogh, Laren

39. THE CHURCH AT NUENEN IN
     WINTER
     Pen and ink on paper; h. 8 1/16, w. 11 3/16 in.
     De la Faille (F) 1238
     Lent by V. W. van Gogh, Laren

40. A COUNTRY ROAD WITH
     POPLARS
     Pen and ink and black crayon on paper; h. 21¼, w. 15⅝ in.
     De la Faille (F) 1239
     Lent by V. W. van Gogh, Laren

41. A PEASANT DIGGING
     Black crayon on paper; h. 21¼, w. 16⅛ in.
     De la Faille (F) 1302
     Lent by V. W. van Gogh, Laren

42. A WOMAN CLEANING A PAN
     Illustrated p. 30. Black crayon on paper; h. 20½, w. 15 15/16 in.
     De la Faille (F) 1282
     Lent by the Kröller-Müller State Museum, Otterlo

43. PEASANTS DIGGING
     Water color and black chalk; h. 7 11/16, w. 12 3/16 in.
     De la Faille (F) 1299
     Lent by the Kröller-Müller State Museum, Otterlo

44. A SHEET OF STUDIES
     Black crayon on paper; h. 13⅜, w. 8 1/16 in.
     De la Faille (F) 1336
     Lent by the Kröller-Müller State Museum, Otterlo

No. 2. The Loom. The Kröller-Müller State Museum

No. 12. Portrait of the Artist. V. W. van Gogh

No. 7. The Potato-Eaters. V. W. van Gogh

No. 26. Vegetable Gardens near the Dunes, The Hague. The Kröller-Müller State Museum

No. 19. Behind the Schenkweg, The Hague. The Kröller-Müller State Museum

No. 27. A View at Scheveningen. V. W. van Gogh

No. 32. The Garden of the Nuenen Vicarage. V. W. van Gogh

No. 35. A Peasant Woman in a White Cap. V. W. van Gogh

No. 34. Studies of Hands. V. W. van Gogh

No. 42. A Woman Cleaning a Pan. The Kröller-Müller State Museum

No. 23. An Old Man. V. W. van Gogh

PARIS

In Paris he shared his brother Theo's flat. At the beginning of his stay he concentrated on restoring his health, almost completely ruined by his previous fasting and bad diet, and most of his teeth had to be removed. He continued carrying out his basic training as he had planned it in Antwerp, by attending an art school run by the painter Cormon, where he applied himself strenuously to working from models and plaster casts. It was there that he met Toulouse-Lautrec and Emile Bernard, who became his friends. As he grew more familiar with the activity of the Parisian art world he came under the influence of the Impressionists and left the school for good.

This was a happy moment for him. Many friends came to visit them at Theo's apartment, and Vincent met the leaders of the new movement in painting, Pissarro, Monet, Seurat, Gauguin, and lived the bohemian life of the artists of the day, working and discussing their problems in the cafés of Montmartre and mingling with writers like Catulle Mendès and Jean Jaurès.

He spent his days painting models and still life or landscapes of Montmartre and the suburbs of Paris, Chatou, Bougival, or Asnières. Emile Bernard says that he would leave his apartment with a large canvas on his back and return with it divided up into small sketches of whatever attracted his attention—the Moulin de la Galette, the bridges over the Seine, or the island of La Grande Jatte. He exhibited in the art shop of Tanguy, the friend of Cézanne and Renoir, and with a group of his friends in the Café du Tambourin, owned by La Segattori, a former model who had posed for Corot and Gérome, and with whom he had a love affair.

The year 1886 saw the eighth and last exhibition of the Impressionists, for whom these were crucial days. The original group, Monet, Pissarro, Renoir, and their friends, who had created the movement and fought its early battles together, was now breaking up. Their basic discovery had come to a dead end. No longer satisfied with spontaneous copying of nature as they saw it, without regard for rules or techniques, they now turned to greater discipline in drawing and painting, and became more interested in the content of their pictures. Under the leadership of Seurat, who had just exhibited his masterpiece La Grande Jatte for the first time, and of Gauguin they followed new tendencies. It was in 1886 that the term Neo-Impressionism was heard for the first time. Vincent had arrived at the dawn of a new period, of which he was to be one of the dominating figures.

Unfortunately, but as was to be expected, this did not last. After a while the difficult aspects of his character reappeared, aggravated by excessive smoking and drinking. He became so irascible, so violent in his arguments that friends began to avoid the apartment because of the constant quarrels. Even his brother, whose patience was certainly beyond reproach, found life with him unbearable. In Theo's letters home he complained of Vincent's strange, dual personality, sometimes sensitive and tender and then suddenly hard, cruel, and egoistic.

In Paris his painting went through a most important change and what can be called the last stage in the formation of his own personal style. This was the result partially of his visits to the Louvre and Luxembourg museums but mostly of his association with the Impressionists. The canvases painted shortly after his arrival are much more luminous than those done in Holland, though the colors are still sober and subdued, as if influenced by Mauve or Corot (see ills. pp. 36, 37). Advised by Pissarro and others, he took up the new method of direct painting without regard for drawing or technique. He became interested in bright pure colors and adopted the small broad strokes and dots which the others used. In these first attempts to follow the new style he seemed to lose much of his individuality, and paintings such as the Woman at the Café du Tambourin (ill. p. 42) or the landscapes of Montmartre are exercises which could have been executed by any member of the group. In his still lives and flowers he maintained his own personality to some extent, and he finally began to assert it again in the self-portrait at an easel. But, on the whole, during the Paris period the influence of Pissarro, Monet, and Seurat predominated, and although he developed his extraordinary sense of color, he concentrated only on the external, the visual aspect of his art, and did not yet combine it with his own very personal feeling for the essential character of the subject. This he was to do in Arles.

P A I N T I N G S

ALL ARE IN OIL ON CANVAS UNLESS OTHERWISE NOTED

45. MONTMARTRE
H. 12⅜, w. 16⅛ in.
De la Faille (H) 261
Lent by V. W. van Gogh, Laren

46. MONTMARTRE
H. 17¾, w. 13⅛ in.
De la Faille (H) 370
Lent by the Art Institute of Chicago

47. PORTRAIT OF THE ARTIST
Oil on pasteboard; h. 7½, w. 5½ in.
De la Faille (H) 418
Lent by V. W. van Gogh, Laren

48. A CORNER OF MONTMARTRE
H. 13¾, w. 25⅜ in.
De la Faille (H) 264
Lent by V. W. van Gogh, Laren

49. A VIEW OF THE BUTTE
MONTMARTRE
H. 16⅞, w. 31½ in.
De la Faille (H) 265
Lent by V. W. van Gogh, Laren

49A. PORTRAIT OF THE ARTIST
H. 16⅛, w. 12⅜ in.
De la Faille (H) 409
Lent by Adelaide Milton de Groot,
New York

Paintings with A following number are shown in New York only.

50. A RESTAURANT AT ASNIERES
Illustrated p. 38. H. 7½, w. 10⅜ in.
De la Faille (H) 365
Lent by V. W. van Gogh, Laren

51. FISHING IN THE SPRING
Illustrated p. 37. H. 19¼, w. 22⅞ in.
De la Faille (H) 367
Lent by Chauncey McCormick, Chicago

52. THE BRIDGE (after Hiroshige)
Illustrated p. 35. H. 28¾, w. 21¼ in.
De la Faille (H) 233
Lent by V. W. van Gogh, Laren

53. A WHEAT FIELD
H. 21¼, w. 25⅝ in.
De la Faille (H) 360
Lent by V. W. van Gogh, Laren

54. A FLOWERPOT WITH HERBS
H. 12⅝, w. 8⅝ in.
De la Faille (H) 315
Lent by V. W. van Gogh, Laren

55. STILL LIFE: FRUIT
Illustrated p. 41. H. 17¾, w. 21½ in.
De la Faille (H) 321
Lent by the Art Institute of Chicago

56. PORTRAIT OF THE ARTIST
Oil on pasteboard; h. 7½, w. 5½ in.
De la Faille (H) 420
Lent by V. W. van Gogh, Laren

57. PORTRAIT OF THE ARTIST
Oil on pasteboard; h. 7½, w. 5½ in.
De la Faille (H) 421
Lent by V. W. van Gogh, Laren

58. LITTLE GARDENS ON THE
BUTTE MONTMARTRE
H. 37¾, w. 47¼ in.
1887. De la Faille (H) pl. IV
Lent by the Municipal Museum, Amsterdam

59. A WOMAN AT THE CAFE DU
TAMBOURIN
Illustrated p. 42. H. 21⅞, w. 18⅛ in.
De la Faille (H) 299
Lent by V. W. van Gogh, Laren

60. SUNFLOWERS
Illustrated p. 40. H. 17, w. 24 in.
De la Faille (H) 278
Lent by the Metropolitan Museum of
Art

61. PORTRAIT OF THE ARTIST
Illustrated p. 43. H. 25⅝, w. 19⅞ in.
1888. De la Faille (H) 425
Lent by V. W. van Gogh, Laren

D R A W I N G S

62. BOULEVARD DE CLICHY, PARIS
Illustrated p. 36. Pen and colored
crayon on paper; h. 14 15/16, w.
20 11/16 in.
De la Faille (F) 1393
Lent by V. W. van Gogh, Laren

63. POTTER'S FIELD, PARIS
Pen and ink, heightened with white, on
paper; h. 14⅜, w. 18⅞ in.
De la Faille (F) 1399
Lent by the Kröller-Müller State Museum, Otterlo

64. FORTIFICATIONS, PARIS
Water color on paper; h. 15 9/16, w.
21 1/16 in.
De la Faille (F) 1400
Lent by V. W. van Gogh, Laren

65. A TEA GARDEN
Illustrated p. 39. Pen and pencil, heightened with white, on gray paper; h.
14¾, w. 19⅞ in.
De la Faille (F) 1407
Lent by V. W. van Gogh, Laren

No. 52. The Bridge (after Hiroshige). V. W. van Gogh

No. 62. Boulevard de Clichy, Paris. V. W. van Gogh

No. 51. Fishing in the Spring. Chauncey McCormick

No. 50. A Restaurant at Asnières. V. W. van Gogh

No. 65. A Tea Garden. V. W. van Gogh

No. 60. Sunflowers. The Metropolitan Museum of Art

No. 55. Still Life: Fruit. The Art Institute of Chicago

No. 59. A Woman at the Café du Tambourin. V. W. van Gogh

No. 61. Portrait of the Artist. V. W. van Gogh

ARLES

Van Gogh's primary reason for leaving Paris for the South was his health. At the end of his stay in Paris he approached some sort of a nervous crisis, which he believed was brought on by the excitement of the city and the abnormal, unhealthy, bohemian life he led there. Arles, once an important city in the Roman Empire and the capital of a kingdom during the Middle Ages, was now a sleepy provincial town basking quietly among the ruins of its former splendor. The sunshine and the pleasant climate there set him back on his feet, and he began the culminating moment of his career. The two years in Paris had matured him, and he now had a more definite idea of what he wanted from life and from his painting. As he looked around him for subjects he was not attracted by the Roman and medieval monuments but by the surrounding country, where spring had begun and there were flowers everywhere in the fields, the gardens, the vineyards, and the orchards. Painting and drawing wherever he went, he explored all the neighboring countryside, visiting the ruins of the abbey of Montmajour and traveling through the Camargue cattle country to the old Phoenician port of Saintes-Maries-de-la-Mer on the shores of the Mediterranean.

Although his concentration on painting brought him great happiness, the conditions in which he lived were in no way improved. He moved from the hotel in which he had settled to a small house where he had a bedroom and studio, but he was as always incapable of living normally. This was due in part to his own unstable character but also to the constant lack of funds. He never seemed to have enough money to satisfy his artistic as well as his personal needs, and when it came to a choice it was invariably the latter which were sacrificed. He fasted sometimes as long as five days, living entirely on coffee and dry bread, and working at the same time with his usual abnormal intensity. The consciousness of his ever increasing debt to his brother and the realization that his paintings never found a buyer (Tersteeg and other dealers had again turned them down) were a constant obsession to him and hung over his life like a dark and threatening cloud.

His loneliness also returned. He had almost no friends outside of Milliet, the Zouave lieutenant (see ill. p. 61), the postman Roulin, and two or three painters whom he neither admired nor felt drawn to. This lack of companionship, from which he always suffered, and his longing for a home made him think again of founding an artistic center, a sort of painters' community where all would share equally and work together under a chosen leader, an "abbot." The center was to be his house, the leader he chose was Gauguin, whom he had met and admired in Paris and who was at that time stranded in Brittany without money. Vincent arranged that in exchange for paintings which would go to his brother in Paris, Gauguin would come to Arles and share his house and living allowance. Working with another painter, and especially one whom he respected and admired as much as Gauguin, was for Vincent the realization of a dream which he had cherished since the early days in Brussels. While awaiting his friend's arrival he did everything to make the house comfortable and especially to decorate it with paintings which Gauguin would admire. He worked feverishly at these and among them are some of his finest works: the Sunflowers in a Vase, the Bedroom, and the Public Gardens (cover and ill. p. 59). He painted the walls yellow, the color of sunlight, so that the atmosphere would always be joyful.

After many delays Gauguin got to Arles on the twentieth of October. At first his presence and companionship had a good effect on Vincent, who shortly before had felt an approaching illness—he had even expressed a fear of madness, comparing himself to Hugo van der Goes, the fifteenth-century Flemish painter who died a lunatic. However, as seemed to be inevitable with him, it was not long before difficulties began. Their discussions degenerated into quarrels and they found themselves in profound disagreement over almost everything. There was nothing astonishing in this, as two men could hardly have been more different. Gauguin was mature and cynical, always planning and theorizing, essentially an intellectual; whereas Van Gogh was spontaneous and almost childishly open-hearted, emotional, and romantic. The tension grew between them until on Christmas Eve Vincent broke under the strain. In a fit of madness he cut off his left ear, took and offered it to a woman in a brothel where he and Gauguin had spent the evening a few days before.

This caused great excitement in the small town. The police were called. Vincent was taken to the hospital. Gauguin telegraphed for Theo to come at once and himself fled to Paris, leaving his belongings behind. After a few days Vincent seemed to have recovered and was allowed to go home. He tried to begin painting again. It was at this time, his head still bandaged, that he did one of his best self-portraits (ill. p. 65). However, Gauguin's desertion and the sight of the desolate, abandoned studio depressed him. The children and the idle of his quarter stood outside of his house and taunted him until he grew excited, screamed, and threw things out of the window. Finally the neighbors sent a petition to the mayor, stating that it was not safe to leave him at liberty and requesting that he be locked up in an institution. He was taken forcibly to the hospital. He suffered renewed attacks and was kept there for several months, during which time he gradually recovered and managed to do some painting. But when the time came for his release he was a broken man; he no longer had the courage to live alone and asked that his brother arrange for him to be interned in an institution where he would be properly cared for and allowed to regain gradually his strength and mental equilibrium.

In spite of the tragedy to which it was a prelude, Vincent's stay in Arles marked the summit of his career as a painter. Liberated from the confusing and overwhelming atmosphere of the capital, he felt free and confident in himself and created his own style. He now decorated his house with his own works, no longer with engravings after his favorite painters. Although he still read many novels and continued to be interested in the painters of the past—with Gauguin he traveled to Montpellier to visit the museum—he was now almost entirely absorbed by his painting and devoted himself to it with a kind of frenzy. He threw off the influence of the Impressionists and other Parisian schools. If he followed anyone during this time it was the Japanese printmaker, but in this case it was rather adaptation and inspiration than direct influence. He admired greatly the simplicity and directness of approach of the Japanese, and to him Provence seemed like the country that he saw in the prints.

He began to work with great intensity and great speed. He compared the painting of a picture with the playing of a part on the stage, in which the actor must think of and co-ordinate innumerable elements all at the same moment. He wrote to his brother that when he was out in the country under the blazing southern sun, he sometimes produced his pictures as if in a trance, almost unconscious of what he was doing. His method was to paint a study on the spot and then another, final, version in the studio.

Many of his best drawings were done at this time. They were executed with a reed cut in the shape of a quill and done in a highly original style inspired by but not imitative of the Japanese. In the paintings of this time the drawing is simpler and clearer than before. Outlines become increasingly important, and certain shapes of strokes are repeated, somewhat in the manner of the Japanese. His touch is no longer like that of Pissarro or Seurat as it was in Paris—repetitious, deliberate, and carefully calculated. The brush strokes now have an instinctive, spontaneous quality, broad in flat surfaces or defining the character of the forms. Color is roughly applied in simple masses and almost always in arbitrarily high intensities. He chose his tones not to correspond with what he saw before him, but rather to emphasize the feeling which he believed to be inherent in his subject. His subjects give an interesting insight into his character and show that although he wanted to paint as a Frenchman, and certainly became a great painter in France, he nevertheless always remained first and foremost a Dutchman. In The Drawbridge (ill. p. 50) he sought out a type of bridge which is comparatively rare in Provence but which is typical in Holland. The Fishing Boats at Saintes-Maries (ill. p. 51) could be on the beach at Scheveningen and the small houses with their thatched roofs also. The Orchards (see color plate and ill. p. 53) no doubt reminded him of Nuenen, the View of La Crau (ill. p. 54) of the great flat stretches of Holland painted by Koninck and Van Goyen. Even the View of Arles with Irises has a freshness which makes one think of Dutch tulips.

His aim was to bring out with simplicity in each painting the human feeling which he believed the subject could express most strongly. As he put it, his desire was to bring consolation to those who are unhappy. He painted La Berceuse as part of a triptych with sunflowers on either side to be put in the cabin of a ship so that when sailors had been many weeks at sea they would think of their homes and the lullabies they had listened to as children. He wanted to express the tenderness and gaiety of the orchards in spring, the feeling of rest in his bedroom, the sinister atmosphere of the Café de Nuit. The self-portrait done just after his first attack has a depth of feeling similar to Rembrandt's.

PAINTINGS

ALL ARE IN OIL ON CANVAS UNLESS OTHERWISE NOTED

66. ALMOND BLOSSOMS
H. 9½, w. 7½ in.
February 1888. De la Faille (H) 427
Lent by V. W. van Gogh, Laren

67. THE DRAWBRIDGE
Illustrated p. 50. H. 23, w. 28¾ in.
March 1888. De la Faille (H) 436
Lent by V. W. van Gogh, Laren

68. THE PINK ORCHARD
H. 25¾, w. 31⅝ in.
March 1888. Intended by the artist to
be hung as a triptych with An Orchard in Bloom and The White Orchard, below. De la Faille (H) 578
Lent by V. W. van Gogh, Laren

69. THE WHITE ORCHARD
Illustrated p. 53. H. 23⅝, w. 31½ in.
March-April 1888. De la Faille (H) 432
Lent by V. W. van Gogh, Laren

70. AN ORCHARD IN BLOOM
Illustrated in color. H. 31⅞, w. 23⅜ in.
April 1888. De la Faille (H) pl. VIII
Lent by V. W. van Gogh, Laren

71. THE BLOSSOMING PEAR TREE
H. 28¾, w. 18⅛ in.
April 1888. De la Faille (H) 434
Lent by V. W. van Gogh, Laren

72. A VIEW OF ARLES WITH IRISES
H. 21¼, w. 25⅝ in.
May 1888. De la Faille (H) 442
Lent by V. W. van Gogh, Laren

73. FISHING BOATS ON THE BEACH
AT SAINTES-MARIES
Illustrated p. 51. H. 25⅝, w. 31⅞ in.
June 1888. De la Faille (H) 451
Lent by V. W. van Gogh, Laren

74. A BUGLER OF THE ZOUAVE
REGIMENT
H. 25⅝, w. 21¼ in.
June 1888. De la Faille (H) 449
Lent by V. W. van Gogh, Laren

75. A VIEW OF SAINTES-MARIES
H. 25¾, w. 21½ in.
June 1888. De la Faille (H) 456
Lent by the Kröller-Müller State Museum, Otterlo

76. A VIEW OF LA CRAU
H. 28½, w. 36¼ in.
June 1888. De la Faille (H) pl. X
Lent by V. W. van Gogh, Laren

77. ROULIN THE POSTMAN
H. 31¼, w. 25 in.
August 1888. De la Faille (H) 461
Lent by the Museum of Fine Arts, Boston

78. SUNFLOWERS IN A VASE
Illustrated in color. H. 37⅜, w. 28¾ in.
August 1888. De la Faille (H) 471
Lent by V. W. van Gogh, Laren

78A. PORTRAIT OF THE ARTIST
(dedicated to Gauguin)
Illustrated p. 60. H. 24⅜, w. 20½ in.
September 1888. De la Faille (H) 505
Lent by Maurice Wertheim, New York

79. THE PUBLIC GARDENS IN ARLES
Illustrated p. 59. H. 28½, w. 35⅝ in.
September 1888. De la Faille (H) 553
Lent by the Phillips Memorial Gallery, Washington, D. C.

80. VAN GOGH'S HOUSE IN ARLES
Illustrated p. 63. H. 29⅞, w. 37 in.
September 1888. De la Faille (H) 489
Lent by V. W. van Gogh, Laren

80A. CAFE DE NUIT
Illustrated p. 58. H. 27½, w. 35 in.
September 1888. De la Faille (H) 491
Lent by Stephen C. Clark, New York

81. PORTRAIT OF LIEUTENANT MILLIET
Illustrated p. 61. H. 23⅝, w. 19¼ in.
September 1888. De la Faille (H) 499
Lent by the Kröller-Müller State Museum, Otterlo

82. A SIDEWALK CAFE AT NIGHT
Illustrated in color. H. 31, w. 24¾ in.
September 1888. De la Faille (H) 493
Lent by the Kröller-Müller State Museum, Otterlo

83. THE GREEN VINEYARD
H. 28, w. 35⅝ in.
October 1888. De la Faille (H) 501
Lent by the Kröller-Müller State Museum, Otterlo

84. WILLOWS AT SUNSET
H. 12¼, w. 13⅜ in.
October 1888. De la Faille (H) 540
Lent by the Kröller-Müller State Museum, Otterlo

85. THE SOWER
H. 13, w. 16⅛ in.
October 1888. De la Faille (H) 480
Lent by V. W. van Gogh, Laren

86. A WALK IN THE ALYSCAMPS PARK
H. 28, w. 35¾ in.
November 1888. De la Faille (H) 513
Lent by the Kröller-Müller State Museum, Otterlo

87. L'ARLESIENNE
(portrait of Madame Ginoux)
Illustrated p. 64. H. 35⅝, w. 28⅜ in.
November 1888. De la Faille (H) 515
Lent by Sam A. Lewisohn, New York

87A. MOTHER ROULIN WITH HER BABY
H. 36¼, w. 28¾ in.
November 1888. De la Faille (H) 520
Lent by Robert Lehman, New York

88. PORTRAIT OF ARMAND ROULIN
H. 25⅝, w. 21¼ in.
November 1888. De la Faille (H) 518
Lent by D. G. van Beuningen, Vierhouten

89. GAUGUIN'S ARMCHAIR
Illustrated in color. H. 35⅝, w. 28⅜ in.
December 1888. De la Faille (H) 522
Lent by V. W. van Gogh, Laren

90. OLEANDERS
H. 23⅝, w. 28¾ in.
1888. De la Faille (H) 594
Lent by Mrs. Charles Suydam Cutting, New York

91. A DRAWING BOARD WITH ONIONS
H. 19⅝, w. 25⅛ in.
January 1889. De la Faille (H) 596
Lent by the Kröller-Müller State Museum, Otterlo

92. THE CRAB
H. 15, w. 17⅞ in.
January 1889. De la Faille (H) 589
Lent by V. W. van Gogh, Laren

93. PORTRAIT OF THE ARTIST WITH A PIPE
Illustrated p. 65. H. 20⅛, w. 17¾ in.
January-February 1889. De la Faille (H) pl. XII
Lent by Mr. and Mrs. Leigh B. Block, Chicago

94. LA BERCEUSE
H. 35¾, w. 28⅛ in.
January-March 1889. De la Faille (H) 527
Lent by the Municipal Museum, Amsterdam

95. A COUNTRY ROAD WITH
    WILLOWS
    Pen and ink and pencil on paper; h.
    10 1/16, w. 13¾ in.
    March 1888. De la Faille (F) 1499
    Lent by V. W. van Gogh, Laren

96. THE WHITE ORCHARD
    Illustrated p. 52. Reed pen, heightened
    with water color, on paper; h. 15 9/16,
    w. 21¼ in.
    April 1888. De la Faille (F) 1414
    Lent by V. W. van Gogh, Laren

97. A VIEW OF LA CRAU
    Illustrated p. 54. Pen and ink on paper;
    h. 18⅞, w. 23⅝ in.
    May 1888. De la Faille (F) 1420
    Lent by V. W. van Gogh, Laren

98. VAN GOGH'S HOUSE IN ARLES
    Illustrated p. 62. Water color and reed
    pen on paper; h. 9⅝, w. 12 in.
    May 1888. De la Faille (F) 1413
    Lent by V. W. van Gogh, Laren

99. THE SOWER
    Illustrated p. 55. Reed pen on paper;
    h. 9 7/16, w. 12⅞ in.
    June 1888. De la Faille (F) 1441
    Lent by V. W. van Gogh, Laren

100. LITTLE HOUSES AT SAINTES-
    MARIES
    Reed pen and ink on paper; h. 11 13/16,
    w. 18½ in.
    June 1888. De la Faille (F) 1438
    Lent by V. W. van Gogh, Laren

101. FISHERMEN'S HOUSES AT
    SAINTES-MARIES
    Reed pen on paper; h. 12, w. 18½ in.
    June 1888. De la Faille (F) 1437
    Lent by V. W. van Gogh, Laren

102. THE WASHERWOMEN
    Illustrated p. 56. Pen and reed pen on
    paper; h. 12 3/16, w. 9 7/16 in.
    June 1888. De la Faille (F) 1444
    Lent by the Kröller-Müller State Mu-
    seum, Otterlo

103. THE ROCK
    Reed pen on paper; h. 19 5/16, w. 24 in.
    July 1888. De la Faille (F) 1447
    Lent by V. W. van Gogh, Laren

104. A BED OF FLOWERS
    Reed pen and ink on paper; h. 24, w.
    19 5/16 in.
    August 1888. De la Faille (F) 1457
    Lent by V. W. van Gogh, Laren

105. A GARDEN WITH THISTLES
    Pen and ink on paper; h. 9⅝, w. 12 9/16
    in.
    October 1888. De la Faille (F) 1466
    Lent by V. W. van Gogh, Laren

106. THE GARDEN OF THE HOSPITAL
    IN ARLES
    Illustrated p. 57. Sepia on paper; h.
    17 15/16, w. 23 3/16 in.
    May 1889. De la Faille (F) 1467
    Lent by V. W. van Gogh, Laren

107. THE BLOSSOMING FRUIT TREE
    Water color on paper; h. 17 15/16, w.
    12 in.
    De la Faille (F) 1469
    Lent by V. W. van Gogh, Laren

108. A LANDSCAPE WITH TELE-
    GRAPH POLES
    Reed pen and ink; h. 9 7/16, w. 12⅞ in.
    De la Faille (F) 1495
    Lent by V. W. van Gogh, Laren

No. 67. The Drawbridge. V. W. van Gogh

No. 73. Fishing Boats on the Beach at Saintes-Maries. V. W. van Gogh

No. 96. The White Orchard (drawing). V. W. van Gogh

No. 69. The White Orchard (painting). V. W. van Gogh

No. 97. A View of La Crau. V. W. van Gogh

No. 99. The Sower. V. W. van Gogh

No. 102. The Washerwomen. The Kröller-Müller State Museum

No. 106. The Garden of the Hospital in Arles. V. W. van Gogh

No. 80A. Café de Nuit. Stephen C. Clark

No. 79. The Public Gardens in Arles. The Phillips Memorial Gallery

No. 78A. Portrait of the Artist. Maurice Wertheim

No. 81. Portrait of Lieutenant Milliet. The Kröller-Müller State Museum

No. 98. Van Gogh's House in Arles (drawing). V. W. van Gogh

No. 80. Van Gogh's House in Arles (painting). V. W. van Gogh

No. 87. L'Arlésienne. Sam A. Lewisohn

No. 70. An Orchard in Bloom. V. W. van Gogh

No. 93. Portrait of the Artist with a Pipe. Mr. and Mrs. Leigh B. Block

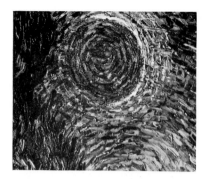

SAINT-RÉMY

After a period of wondering whether he should move to another house in a different part of Arles, go to Brittany to join Gauguin and the group of artists with him at Pont-Aven, or return to Paris, Vincent and his brother decided he needed above all a quiet, well-ordered daily life and that the best place to find this would be the Asylum of Saint Paul near the town of Saint-Rémy, about twenty kilometers from Arles. This institution still exists and is in use to this day. It is located in the remains of a twelfth-century monastery, situated at the foot of a small range of hills, in a fertile plain of wheat fields and olive groves. In the distance, on the horizon, can be seen the ancient city of Avignon and the Alps. An avenue of tall pine trees leads to the entrance, and it is surrounded by a large abandoned park, full of flowers.

In 1889 the buildings were divided into men's and women's wards. The former occupied a long, austere wing made up of a corridor with many small cells looking out on the garden. The inmates were taken care of by nuns and wardens. They were divided into three classes according to the price they paid for their board and lodging: Vincent was in the third class. He had a room to sleep in and another for painting. He did not like the food—there were sometimes cockroaches in it—and, except for the periods which followed his attacks, when he was on a special diet, he took only soup and bread.

The director of the institution was a former naval surgeon, who had chosen this post as an easy one in which to spend his declining years. He treated Vincent kindly, allowing him to paint in the surrounding country and even to make occasional trips to Arles to see his old friends. The superior of the nuns was less lenient, but she was perhaps the only one who admired Vincent's paintings. The other inmates never came into close contact with him. At first he did not mind them, in spite of their screams and moans, which sometimes went on all night. The fact that it was shared by others made him see his own disease in a more normal light. But gradually as he lost hope for his own recovery, he grew afraid of them and became obsessed with the idea that their proximity contributed to his condition.

He spent twelve months at Saint-Rémy, and during this time he had serious attacks at intervals of about two to three months. When he arrived he was in full possession of his senses and himself explained his case to the director, describing what had happened at Arles and telling of what he believed to be hereditary aspects of the disease in his family. He continued in this state for some time, gradually getting back his health and strength to such an extent that he almost believed himself cured. He obtained permission to go to Arles for a day to attend to the belongings he had left there; and then suddenly, a few days after this, the disease struck again. He lost his mind and suffered from the effects of the attack for several weeks. This was followed by a period of extreme depression and despair; he again picked up but only to succumb again at the moment when he least expected it. This process of recovery followed by a relapse became chronic, so that he lived in fear of the disease and found his only moments of peace and balance in his painting. Many controversial opinions have been written about the illness that afflicted him since the doctor at Saint-Rémy first diagnosed it as epilepsy, but whatever its nature one aspect of it is significant; in between the attacks he became normal again and was able to produce paintings equal in quality to the best he had done before.

After the last attack, which occurred during a trip to Arles, he became obsessed with the desire to leave the asylum and go somewhere in the North where he could be in contact with other artists again. He attributed his religious hallucinations to spending so much time in buildings which had formerly been monasteries (this was also true of the hospital at Arles) and became very strongly opposed to the nuns at Saint-Rémy, who he said encouraged such aberrations instead of trying to cure them. His antipathy to them was increased by their forbidding him to paint oustide of the building and he even asked to be removed to a secular asylum, or, if this should be impossible, to be allowed to join the Foreign Legion.

Considering his illness and the fact that he was living in an asylum surrounded by lunatics, Vincent's painting suffered very little during this time. He always kept up his interest in what the other painters were doing in Paris. During the initial period of discouragement he did very little, but gradually as he grew stronger the old fire returned. When he realized that he would perhaps never recover, he worked feverishly, to use his own words, like a miner who knows that his life is always in danger. What most astonished the people at the asylum was the speed with which he painted. His color changed somewhat, from the bright Japanese-like tones to more subdued harmonies dominated in general by ochers. The stylization and use of outline which had begun to appear at Arles, particularly in his portraits, became more emphatic, and he tried consciously to give his drawing the character of early wood engraving. At first his brush strokes continued to be violent and expressive, and he applied his paint in abnormally heavy layers after the manner of Monticelli, whom he continued to admire (see frontispiece), but when he isolated himself completely and remained alone for long periods he painted more thinly (see ill. p. 74).

His choice of subjects reflected his state of mind. At first he painted what he saw around him: the view from his window, the garden, the corridor of the asylum, the portraits of the chief warder and his wife. When he was allowed out, he worked in the street of the village of Saint-Rémy and found many new subjects in the wheat fields, the olive orchards, the cypresses, and the flowers (see color plate and ills. pp. 75, 80,

83, 81). Again it is significant that he concentrated on nature as he had always done and showed no interest whatever in the ruins of a Roman triumphal arch and a so-called mausoleum of the Julii near by.

From the time of the first attack in Arles his homesickness and longing for everything that reminded him of his youth and Holland gradually increased. When he was confined to his room because of illness or because bad weather made it impossible to work outside, he often drew from memory scenes from the life of the Brabant peasants (see ills. pp. 78, 79, 85) or made paintings based on earlier drawings. He also copied engravings after Rembrandt, Millet, and Delacroix, producing his own very personal interpretations of their works, for which he improvised the colors, partly from his memory of their general harmonies and partly according to what he felt was most expressive in the subject (see ill. p. 82). These give us a most unusual key to his way of feeling.

Except for one or two short moments of happiness such as that occasioned by his brother's marriage and the birth of his nephew, a deep sadness dominates all this period and is communicated by the paintings. Recognition of his talent began to appear during the early part of the year 1890; but even this did not seem to lift up his spirit. He was invited by a group of Belgian artists who called themselves "the Twenty" to exhibit several paintings in Brussels, among them the Sunflowers and the Orchard in Bloom (see color plate). When one of these was sold he saw in it no cause for rejoicing. At about the same time Albert Aurier, a young critic, published an article praising his work in a Paris magazine. Even this seemed to leave him almost indifferent. He considered it exaggerated, and with characteristic modesty and loyalty to his fellow artists he wrote to Aurier telling him how much he owed to Monticelli and to his friend Gauguin.

PAINTINGS

ALL ARE IN OIL ON CANVAS UNLESS OTHERWISE NOTED

109. THE ONE-EYED MAN
H. 22, w. 14⅛ in.
1889. De la Faille (H) 559
Lent by V. W. van Gogh, Laren

110. A LANDSCAPE WITH PLOWED
FIELDS
H. 28, w. 35⅝ in.
May 1889. De la Faille (H) 739
Lent by Robert Oppenheimer, San
Francisco

111. THE HOSPITAL GARDEN AT
SAINT-REMY
H. 37⅞, w. 29⅜ in.

May-June 1889. De la Faille (H) 741
Lent by the Kröller-Müller State Museum, Otterlo

111A. THE STARRY NIGHT
H. 28¾, w. 36¼ in.
June 1889. De la Faille (H) 612
Lent by the Museum of Modern Art,
New York (acquired through the Lillie P. Bliss Bequest)

112. CYPRESSES
Illustrated in color. H. 36¾, w. 29⅛ in.
June 1889. De la Faille (H) 616
Lent by the Metropolitan Museum of
Art

113. CYPRESSES WITH TWO FIGURES
Illustrated p. 83. H. 16½, w. 10¼ in.
June 1889. De la Faille (H) 618
Lent by V. W. van Gogh, Laren

114. THE WOODCUTTER (after Millet)
H. 17⅛, w. 9⅞ in.
August-November 1889. De la Faille (H) 689
Lent by V. W. van Gogh, Laren

115. SHEEPSHEARERS (after Millet)
H. 16⅞, w. 11⅜ in.
August-November 1889. De la Faille (H) 646
Lent by V. W. van Gogh, Laren

116. THE SHEAF-BINDER (after Millet)
H. 17¼, w. 12¾ in.
August-November 1889. De la Faille (H) 681
Lent by V. W. van Gogh, Laren

117. VAN GOGH'S BEDROOM IN ARLES
Illustrated p. 73. H. 28⅜, w. 35⅝ in.
September 1889. De la Faille (H) 627
Lent by V. W. van Gogh, Laren

118. PIETA (after Delacroix)
Illustrated p. 82. H. 28¾, w. 23¾ in.
September 1889. De la Faille (H) 625
Lent by V. W. van Gogh, Laren

119. PORTRAIT OF THE ARTIST
Illustrated p. 72. H. 22⅜, w. 17⅛ in.
September 1889. De la Faille (H) 624
Lent by John Hay Whitney, New York

120. AN OLIVE ORCHARD
Illustrated p. 75. H. 28, w. 35⅜ in.
September-October 1889. De la Faille (H) 708
Lent by the Kröller-Müller State Museum, Otterlo

121. A STUDY OF FIR TREES
H. 16⅞, w. 19¼ in.
October-November 1889. De la Faille (H) 744
Lent by the Kröller-Müller State Museum, Otterlo

122. FIR WOODS IN THE EVENING
H. 35⅜, w. 28 in.
October-November 1889. De la Faille (H) 573
Lent by the Kröller-Müller State Museum, Otterlo

123. THE ROAD-MENDERS
Illustrated p. 74. H. 29⅛, w. 36⅝ in.
November 1889. De la Faille (H) 667
Lent by the Cleveland Museum of Art

124. THE ENCLOSED FIELD
H. 28, w. 35⅞ in.
November 1889. De la Faille (H) 662
Lent by the Kröller-Müller State Museum, Otterlo

125. THE RAVINE
H. 28¾, w. 36¼ in.
December 1889. De la Faille (H) 670
Lent by the Kröller-Müller State Museum, Otterlo

126. A MEADOW IN THE MOUNTAINS
H. 28⅜, w. 35¾ in.
December 1889. De la Faille (H) 730
Lent by the Kröller-Müller State Museum, Otterlo

127. THE FIRST STEPS (after Millet)
H. 28¾, w. 36¼ in.
January-February 1890. De la Faille (H) 685
Lent anonymously

128. THE PLOW (after a drawing by Millet)
Illustrated p. 77. H. 28⅜, w. 36¼ in.
January-February 1890. De la Faille (H) 686
Lent by V. W. van Gogh, Laren

129. A WINTER LANDSCAPE
H. 11⅜, w. 14⅜ in.
April 1890. De la Faille (H) 693
Lent by V. W. van Gogh, Laren

130. ON THE THRESHOLD OF ETERNITY
Illustrated p. 79. H. 31½, w. 25¼ in.
May 1890. De la Faille (H) 719
Lent by the Kröller-Müller State Museum, Otterlo

131. A ROAD WITH CYPRESSES
H. 35¾, w. 28 in.
May 1890. De la Faille (H) 695
Lent by the Kröller-Müller State Museum, Otterlo

132. IRISES
Illustrated p. 81. H. 36¼, w. 29 in.
May 1890. De la Faille (H) 700
Lent by V. W. van Gogh, Laren

133. TREE TRUNKS
H. 28¾, w. 35⅞ in.
May 1890. De la Faille (H) 697
Lent by the Kröller-Müller State Museum, Otterlo

134. THE RESURRECTION OF LAZARUS (after Rembrandt)
Illustrated p. 76. H. 19⅛, w. 24¾ in.
May 1890. De la Faille (H) 699
Lent by V. W. van Gogh, Laren

DRAWINGS

135. A PEACOCK MOTH
Black crayon and ink; h. 5⅞, w. 9⅝ in.
May 1889. De la Faille (F) 1523
Lent by V. W. van Gogh, Laren

136. CYPRESSES
Illustrated p. 80. Reed pen and ink on paper; h. 24⅝, w. 18½ in.
June 1889. De la Faille (F) 1525
Lent by the Brooklyn Museum

137. THE FOUNTAIN IN THE HOSPITAL GARDEN
Illustrated p. 84. Pen and ink on paper; h. 18⅞, w. 17 11/16 in.
De la Faille (F) 1531
Lent by V. W. van Gogh, Laren

138. A PARK
Water color on paper; h. 17½, w. 24⅝ in.
De la Faille (F) 1533
Lent by V. W. van Gogh, Laren

139. A CYPRESS AND A FLOWERING TREE
Pen and ink and pencil; h. 18½, w. 24⅝ in.
De la Faille (F) 1538
Lent by V. W. van Gogh, Laren

140. A PATH IN THE PINES
Black crayon on paper; h. 7⅞, w. 11⅜ in.
De la Faille (F) 1582
Lent by V. W. van Gogh, Laren

141. THE GIG
Black crayon on paper; h. 11, w. 9⅝ in.
De la Faille (F) 1587
Lent by V. W. van Gogh, Laren

142. PEASANTS AT DINNER
Illustrated p. 85. Charcoal and pencil on paper; h. 13⅜, w. 19 11/16 in.
De la Faille (F) 1588
Lent by V. W. van Gogh, Laren

143. A WINTER LANDSCAPE WITH FIGURES
Pencil on paper; h. 9 1/16, w. 12 3/16 in.
De la Faille (F) 1592
Lent by V. W. van Gogh, Laren

144. A LANDSCAPE AT SAINT-REMY
Black crayon on paper; h. 12⅜, w. 9 7/16 in.
De la Faille (F) 1593
Lent by V. W. van Gogh, Laren

145. A WINDOW OF THE HOSPITAL AT SAINT-REMY
Illustrated p. 71. Water color, oil, and charcoal on paper; h. 24, w. 18½ in.
De la Faille (F) 1528
Lent by V. W. van Gogh, Laren

146. FLOWERING STEMS
Pen and ink on paper; h. 16⅛, w. 12 3/16 in.
De la Faille (F) 1612
Lent by V. W. van Gogh, Laren

147. A GARDEN WITH A STONE BENCH
Reed pen and ink; h. 24⅝, w. 18½ in.
May 1889. De la Faille (F) 1522
Lent by V. W. van Gogh, Laren

No. 145. A Window of the Hospital at Saint-Rémy. V. W. van Gogh

No. 119. Portrait of the Artist. John Hay Whitney

No. 117. Van Gogh's Bedroom in Arles. V. W. van Gogh

No. 123. The Road-Menders. The Cleveland Museum of Art

No. 120. An Olive Orchard. The Kröller-Müller State Museum

No. 134. The Resurrection of Lazarus (after Rembrandt). V. W. van Gogh

No. 128. The Plow (after Millet). V. W. van Gogh

No. 24. On the Threshold of Eternity (drawing). V. W. van Gogh

No. 130. On the Threshold of Eternity (painting). The Kröller-Müller State Museum

No. 136. Cypresses. The Brooklyn Museum

No. 112. Cypresses. The Metropolitan Museum of Art

No. 132. Irises. V. W. van Gogh

82

No. 118. Pietà (after Delacroix). V. W. van Gogh

No. 113. Cypresses with Two Figures. V. W. van Gogh

No. 137. The Fountain in the Hospital Garden. V. W. van Gogh

No. 142. Peasants at Dinner. V. W. van Gogh

AUVERS

Meanwhile his brother, on the advice of Pissarro, had arranged for him to go to Auvers, a village in the northern suburbs of Paris, where a certain Dr. Gachet, who had been a friend of Cézanne and the Impressionists, would take care of him. Vincent arrived in Paris on the morning of Sunday the seventeenth of May, 1890. His brother fetched him at the station and took him straight to his apartment near the Place Pigalle in Montmartre. There for the first time he met his sister-in-law and saw the baby, who had been named after him. He stayed with them three days, during which he spent most of his time studying the paintings that had accumulated during his absence. The apartment was full of them, hanging on the walls—The Potato-Eaters in the dining room, The Orchard in Bloom in the bedroom, and others in the closets, under the bed, in every available space. Vincent would spread them out on the floor and contemplate them for hours. For him it was like reading back through the story of his life as an artist.

His brother's home had again become a meeting place for the young artists whose work he tried to sell. He had only recently organized a show for Pissarro. Many of his friends came to see Vincent, who once more found himself in the circle of painters he had known two years before. But the excitement quickly tired him, and, driven by the desire to begin working again, he left Paris for Auvers.

On arriving, Vincent took a room in a small inn located not far from the Town Hall, which he was to paint, decorated for the national holiday (see ill. p. 95). Dr. Gachet met him and they quickly became friends. Vincent wrote to his brother that he knew at once that the doctor and he suffered from the same complaint. Gachet was in the employ of a French railroad company. He had a clinic in Paris, where he worked several days a week. The rest of the time he spent in Auvers, at his favorite pastime, painting, for he was an amateur painter and engraver of some standing, signing his works P. van Ryssel. He exhibited at the Salon des Independants, and had many friends among the new school of painters. Cézanne, Pissarro, Renoir, Sisley, Guillaumain all came to visit him, and he bought their pictures to decorate his house. He had even known men whom Vincent had always admired such as Corot, Daumier, and Monticelli.

He encouraged Vincent greatly in his work, frequently coming to see him and discussing his problems. They made etchings and printed them together on his press.

Vincent painted still lives in the house and did portraits of the doctor and his daughter. He was conscious of a new confidence gained in the South, and his new surroundings appealed to him both by contrast and because they reminded him somewhat of
Holland: the little village with its thatched cottages nestling in the valley of the Oise,
the charming river, the wooded hills, the gardens, the wheat fields, and the vineyards.
Theo visited him with his family, and they spent a happy day together, Vincent playing with the baby and taking long walks in the country with them.

His work at Auvers confirmed and accentuated the tendencies which had appeared
at Saint-Rémy. The drawing continued to be broad and simple, the outlines in exaggerated curves like early woodcuts. His brush stroke grew even more vital and confident, playing a more important role in the definition of form. It acquired more personality, was larger in scale, and thus became even more expressive than before. In a
sense it had an abstract life of its own. The color harmonies grew cooler under the
influence of the northern landscape. In addition to the old contrasts of complemen-
taries he now sought combinations of vibrating blues and greens. His subjects remained the same, the fields stretching out before him and views of the peasant houses
among the trees. He also made close-up studies of plants—wheat sheaves, tree roots,
flowers—and used them as backgrounds for his portraits. On the whole his painting
became more definitely stylized. Everything in his canvases seems to be moving, living; the views of the fields seem to be swelling like great waves (see ills. p. 93), and
his plant studies have a jungle-like feeling of constant growth. In most of the pictures
the mood is sad, as in the portrait of Gachet, where he wanted to paint a "heartbreak-
ing expression."

Trouble began again shortly after his family's visit. The baby became seriously ill,
and at the same time his brother again considered the possibility of breaking with the
the firm of Goupil and starting a business of his own. This would have meant a reduced income for him and consequently also for Vincent. Vincent went to Paris to
discuss it, but the visit was an unhappy one because his brother and his wife were dis-
traught about the baby and he himself badly affected by the general excitement. On
that day Toulouse-Lautrec lunched with him, and Guillaumain was expected later.
But in spite of Vincent's desire to see the latter, he left hurriedly for the country, fear-
ing the consequences of the nervous state he already was in. From that time his state
of mind became more and more depressed; he had violent outbreaks of temper and
caused scenes for trivial reasons at the Gachets. Afterwards he would go off and
wander alone across the fields, talking to himself. His painting reflected this, be-
coming more violent and gloomy, as in the extraordinary and almost prophetic Crows
over the Wheat Fields (ill. p. 93), which was his last work.

Finally he gave up the struggle, overcome by his sense of guilt at being a perpetual
financial burden to his brother, by the loneliness which he had tried all his life to
escape and to which his illness now condemned him, and by the fear of the attacks
which he now knew would return to strike him down again and again. On the twenty-
seventh of July, 1890, at the age of thirty-seven, he went out to a lonely field behind

the Manor of Auvers and shot himself. The wound was not fatal, and so he returned to his room in the inn and lay on his bed, face to the wall, awaiting death. He was found there by the innkeeper, who called Gachet. The doctor examined him and, finding that the bullet could not be removed, administered first aid and decided to await developments. He asked Vincent for his brother's address but got no answer. Vincent asked only if he might have his pipe and on being given it, smoked in silence. When Theo was reached and arrived the next morning he said: "I did it for the good of all." During the day he talked about his misery, his loneliness, asked often for Theo's wife and baby, but was indifferent to any hope of recovery. He died early in the morning of the twenty-ninth. His last words were: "I wish I could die now."

A few friends came to his funeral. He was buried in the little cemetery of Auvers on the hill above the village, near the wheat fields, the woods, and the flowers which he had always loved.

The shock of his death was too much for Theo. His mind was affected, and six months later he died insane, in Holland. His body was brought to France, and he was buried next to his brother.

P A I N T I N G S

ALL ARE IN OIL ON CANVAS UNLESS OTHERWISE NOTED

148. CHESTNUT TREES IN FLOWER
Illustrated p. 90. H. 27½, w. 22¾ in.
May 1890. De la Faille (H) 749
Lent by Mr. and Mrs. George Gard
DeSylva, through the Los Angeles
County Museum

149. UNDERGROWTH
H. 19⅝, w. 39⅜ in.
June 1890. De la Faille (H) 764
Lent anonymously

149A. PORTRAIT OF DOCTOR
GACHET
Illustrated p. 91. H. 26, w. 22⅜ in.
June 1890. De la Faille (H) 752
Lent by Siegfried Kramarsky, New
York

150. THE AUVERS STAIRS
Illustrated p. 92. H. 18⅞, w. 27½ in.

June 1890. De la Faille (H) 783
Lent by the City Art Museum, St. Louis

151. THE TOWN HALL OF AUVERS ON
THE FOURTEENTH OF JULY
Illustrated p. 95. H. 28⅜, w. 36⅝ in.
July 1890. De la Faille (H) pl. XVI
Lent by Mr. and Mrs. Leigh B. Block,
Chicago

152. A FIELD UNDER A STORMY SKY
Illustrated p. 93. H. 19⅜, w. 39⅜ in.
July 1890. De la Faille (H) 806
Lent by V. W. van Gogh, Laren

153. CROWS OVER THE WHEAT
FIELDS
Illustrated p. 93. H. 19⅞, w. 39½ in.
July 1890. De la Faille (H) 809
Lent by V. W. van Gogh, Laren

No. 148. Chestnut Trees in Flower. Mr. and Mrs. George Gard DeSylva

No. 149ᴀ. Portrait of Doctor Gachet. Siegfried Kramarsky

No. 150. The Auvers Stairs. The City Art Museum, St. Louis

No. 152. A Field Under a Stormy Sky. V. W. van Gogh

No. 153. Crows Over the Wheat Fields. V. W. van Gogh

No. 157. The Town Hall of Auvers on the Fourteenth of July (drawing). V. W. van Gogh

No. 151. The Town Hall of Auvers on the Fourteenth of July. Mr. and Mrs. Leigh B. Block

No. 156. Houses at Auvers. V. W. van Gogh